Arctic Fox Pups

by Ruth Owen

Consultants:

Suzy Gazlay, M.A.
Recipient, Presidential Award
for Excellence in Science Teaching

Dr. Maarten Loonen
University of Groningen, Arctic Centre

BEARPORT
PUBLISHING

New York, New York

Credits

Cover, © Yva Momatiuk & John Eastcott/Minden Pictures/FLPA; 4–5, © National Geographic/Superstock; 6–7, © Michio Hoshino/Minden Pictures/FLPA; 8–9, © IndexStock/Superstock; 9T, © All Canada Photos/Superstock; 10, © Michael Gore/FLPA; 11, © age fotostock/Superstock; 12–13, © ecoventurestravel/Shutterstock; 14, © Erwin and Peggy Bauer/Bruce Coleman Photography; 15, © Bart Breet/fotonatura.com/FLPA; 16–17, © Richard Kemp/Oxford Scientific Photo Library; 17T, © Jasper Doest/Minden Pictures/FLPA; 18, © Harri Taavetti/FLPA; 19T, © Science Faction/Superstock; 19B, © Matthias Breiter/Minden Pictures/FLPA; 20B, © Stefan Huwiler/Rolf Nussbaumer Photography/Alamy; 20–21, © Sam Chadwick/Shutterstock; 22C, © ecoventurestravel/Shutterstock; 22B, © National Geographic/Superstock; 23C, © Visuals Unlimited/Naturepl; 23B, © Jasper Doest/Minden Pictures/FLPA.

Publisher: Kenn Goin
Senior Editor: Lisa Wiseman
Creative Director: Spencer Brinker
Design: Alix Wood
Photo Researcher: Ruby Tuesday Books Ltd

Library of Congress Cataloging-in-Publication Data

Owen, Ruth, 1967–
  Arctic fox pups / by Ruth Owen.
      p. cm. — (Wild baby animals)
  Includes bibliographical references and index.
  ISBN-13: 978-1-61772-156-4 (library binding)
  ISBN-10: 1-61772-156-5 (library binding)
  1. Arctic fox—Infancy—Juvenile literature. I. Title.
  QL737.C22O965 2011
  599.776'4139—dc22
                                        2010041245

For more information, write to Bearport Publishing Company, Inc., 101 Fifth Avenue, Suite 6R, New York, New York 10003. Printed in the United States of America in North Mankato, Minnesota.

122010
10810CGE

10 9 8 7 6 5 4 3 2 1

Contents

Meet the pups

Five arctic fox **pups** peek out from some rocks.

The pups are about five weeks old.

They live in a cozy underground home.

They live with their mother and father.

Underground home

Arctic fox pups

5

Where do arctic foxes live?

Arctic foxes live near the **North Pole**.

This part of the world is called the **Arctic**.

That is how the foxes got their name.

The Arctic is one of the coldest places on Earth.

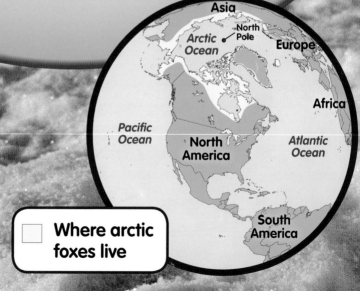

Asia

North Pole

Arctic Ocean

Europe

Africa

Pacific Ocean

North America

Atlantic Ocean

South America

☐ **Where arctic foxes live**

7

Arctic fox fur

In winter, the adult fox's white fur blends in with the snow.

This helps the fox hide from polar bears and wolves that hunt it.

Winter fur

In summer, the fox's fur turns brown or grayish-brown.

The summer fur is thin so the fox stays cool.

Summer fur

Arctic fox homes

Arctic foxes dig underground homes called **dens**.

The dens have rooms where the foxes sleep.

The foxes use small tunnels to get from one part of the den to another.

Den

Arctic fox pup

13

Mothers and pups

A mother arctic fox gives birth in a den.

A **litter** may have 5 pups or more.

Some litters have as many as
15 or 20 pups!

Litter

Some pups have white and gray fur.

Others have brown or grayish-brown fur.

Arctic fox pups drink milk from their mother's body.

Mother fox

Pups feeding

Caring for the pups

The pups start going outside when they are about three weeks old.

At that time, they start to eat meat, too.

At first, the parents bring meat to the pups.

Meat

They also teach the pups how to hunt.

Soon the little foxes will be able to find their own meat.

Mother fox

Pups

Arctic fox food

Arctic foxes eat berries and insects.

They also hunt for small animals such as lemmings.

A lemming

The foxes have very good hearing.

They can hear animals under the snow.

They jump up and
dive into the snow
to grab their **prey**.

Growing up

Some young arctic foxes stay with their parents for a year or more.

They help care for new pups.

One-year-old female fox

New pups

Most young foxes, however, leave home when they are about ten months old.

They are now ready to begin their grown-up lives!

Glossary

Arctic (ARK-tik) the northernmost area on Earth; it includes the Arctic Ocean, the North Pole, and northern parts of Europe, Asia, and North America

North Pole

North America

Atlantic Ocean

Pacific Ocean

Africa

South America

Australia

The area shaded in white is the Arctic.

dens (DENZ) homes where wild animals can rest, hide from enemies, and have babies

litter (LIT-ur) a group of baby animals that are born to the same mother at the same time

North Pole

North Pole
(NORTH POHL)
the northernmost
point on Earth

prey (PRAY) animals
that are hunted by
other animals for food

pups (PUHPS)
the babies of
some animals,
such as arctic
foxes and seals

Index

Read more

Sisk, Maeve T. *Arctic Foxes (Animals That Live in the Tundra).* New York: Gareth Stevens (2010).

Stuhr, Carri. *Arctic Foxes (Early Bird Nature Books).* Minneapolis, MN: Lerner (2009).

Townsend, Emily Rose. *Arctic Foxes.* Mankato, MN: Capstone (2004).

Learn more online

To learn more about arctic foxes, visit **www.bearportpublishing.com/WildBabyAnimals**

About the author

Ruth Owen has been writing children's books for more than ten years. She lives in Cornwall, England, just minutes from the ocean. Ruth loves gardening and caring for her family of llamas.